Text © 2006 Lane Walker Foard
Illustrations © 2006 Elvis Swift

ISBN 0-8118-5276-8

Design by NOON / www.designatnoon.com
Illustrations by Elvis Swift
Manufactured in China

Chronicle Books endeavors to use environmentally responsible paper
in its gift and stationery products.

Distributed in Canada by
Raincoast Books
9050 Shaughnessy Street
Vancouver, B.C. V6P 6E5

10 9 8 7 6 5 4 3 2 1

Chronicle Books LLC
85 Second Street
San Francisco, CA 94105
www.chroniclebooks.com

This book is a product of the mind of Lane Walker Foard, who is currently the recognized leader
of Squibnocket Cards—the copy–heavy greeting cards that have been unintentionally consequen-
tial since 1999. Lane resides with his wife and two sons in Portland, Oregon.

THE NEWLYWEDS'
BOOK OF FIRSTS
A KEEPSAKE JOURNAL

BY LANE WALKER FOARD

CHRONICLE BOOKS
SAN FRANCISCO

AND SO IT IS . . .

you have become married. You have closed the windows and turned out the lights on your single lives. You have moved in, pushed the twin beds together, and jointly started your mail-order-cataloged living room. You have publicly and legally chosen to focus your inclination on a single person. Forever until death. Yessiree, these are the salad days. And hard work and good fortune willing, they will never end. But never are the salad days crisper and more tasty than during the first year before the sweet anesthetic of newlywed bliss wears off. This book will chronicle all the new things that you do, experience, and observe as "Husband" and "Wife," so that fifty years later, when you're still holding hands on the front porch swing, you can pull this out, reminisce and say something heartfelt like, "Wow, look at us there, married 24 hours and still happy."

FOR US   FOR HER   FOR HIM

THE FIRST TIME WE WERE WALKING DOWN THE STREET, IN OUR PERMANENTLY smiling, love-intoxicated, newlywed-addled stupor, and one of us asked, "Do you think we'll still hold hands when we're fifty?"

DATE _____ 20 _____

THE FIRST TIME WE REALIZED WE COULD NO LONGER USE THE ALL-POWERFUL, untrumpable, "I can't possibly deal with that right now—I'm planning a wedding" line anymore.

DATE _____ 20 _____

THE FIRST TIME I PUBLICLY INTRODUCED HIM AS MY HUSBAND AND FELT LIKE IT
should be punctuated by heralding trumpets, wild applause, and confetti falling
from the ceiling.

DATE _____ 20 _____

THE FIRST TIME I REALIZED THAT THE SPACE FOR VISUAL RECALL IN MY BRAIN
that usually stores images of, say, the subtle differences between the grille of a '65
Mustang and the grille of a '66 Mustang or, say, Michael Jordan's final shot will also
now and forever hold the sight of my bride walking down the aisle.

DATE _____ 20 _____

THE FIRST TIME WE REALIZED WE HAD JUST ENGAGED IN A LONGER-THAN-IS-
socially-acceptable and few-degrees-more-than-romantic kiss on aisle seven in the
grocery store, confirming that the sweet anesthetic of newlywed bliss had not yet
worn off.

DATE _____ 20 _____

THE FIRST TIME WE STARTED TO TAKE A CEREMONIAL BITE OF THE WEDDING
cake we'd saved in the freezer, until we realized that it had been in there for, as
tradition would have it, an entire year.

DATE _____ 20 _____

THE FIRST TIME WE RAN INTO (AND HAD AN ENTIRELY UNCOMFORTABLE "SO, HOW was the wedding?" conversation with) someone who didn't quite make the cut for our wedding invitations.

DATE _____ 20 _____

THE FIRST TIME ONE OF US GOT A PERPLEXINGLY RANDOM PHONE CALL FROM an old, out-of-touch high school classmate (who was apparently in town, single, and suddenly frisky), only to have the call end abruptly and awkwardly after the dropping of the "Well, I'm married now" conversation cluster bomb.

DATE _____ 20 _____

THE FIRST TIME I LEARNED SHE HAD CHANGED HER ATM PIN

to our wedding date.

DATE _____ 20 _____

THE FIRST TIME I LEARNED HIS ATM PIN AND REALIZED HE CHOSE THE NUMBER

for something slightly appalling yet somehow forgivably masculine, such as the year he lost his virginity.

DATE _____ 20 _____

WIFE'S FORGED VERSION OF HUSBAND'S SIGNATURE ● ●

HUSBAND'S SIGNATURE ● ●

HUSBAND'S FORGED VERSION OF WIFE'S SIGNATURE ● ●

WIFE'S SIGNATURE ● ●

THE ART OF FORGERY

THE FIRST TIME ONE OF US HAD TO FORGE THE OTHER'S SIGNATURE AND WAS ABLE to suppress the internal feelings of criminality and fears of federal prosecution and hard time with the simple thought, "You know what? I'm unofficially allowed to do this—we're married."

DATE _____ 2 0 _____

....

....

....

THE FIRST TIME ONE OF US EMPLOYED THE "YOU GOT TO HAVE YOUR . . ." line of persuasion, as in, "You got to have your stupendously large gas grill that can be seen from outer space, so I should get to have my own vanity sink."

DATE _____ 2 0 _____

....

....

....

THE FIRST TIME I REALIZED THE FACT THAT I KNOW SOMETHING MINIMAL AND peculiar and identifiable about my spouse's body (a birthmark, a scar, whatever) makes me feel more connected and married than any ceremony or ring or fancy wedding dress ever could.

DATE _____ 20 _____

THE FIRST TIME I GOT THAT "WOW, I'M REALLY DOING THIS HUSBAND THING" feeling at a restaurant when my wife was in the bathroom and I both knew and remembered to order her a vodka tonic with a splash of lime juice.

DATE _____ 20 _____

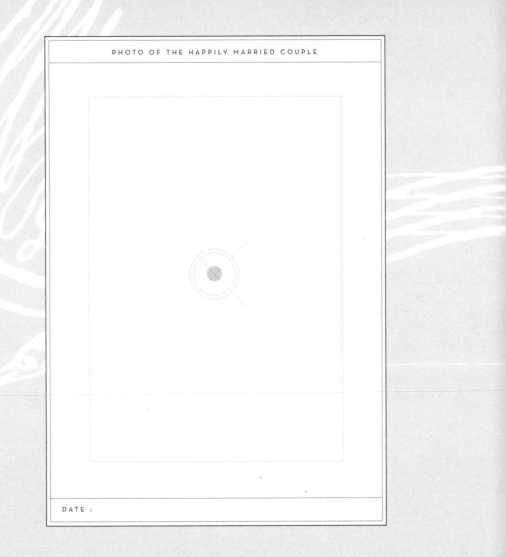

PHOTO OF THE HAPPILY MARRIED COUPLE

DATE :

THE FIRST TIME I REALIZED THAT SPENDING SOME QUALITY ONE-ON-ONE TIME (shopping or driving home from the airport or going to a Chippendales performance) with my new mother-in-law is slightly less like one of Dante's inner circles of hell than I imagined it might be (at least until the grandchildren are born).

DATE _____ 20 _____

....
....
....

THE FIRST TIME I REALIZED THAT SPENDING SOME QUALITY ONE-ON-ONE TIME (going to the hardware store or driving home from the airport or watching the game) with my new father-in-law is remarkably less like one of Dante's inner circles of hell than I imagined it might be (at least until my first moment of unemployment comes).

DATE _____ 20 _____

....
....
....

THE FIRST TIME WE BOTH STRATEGICALLY CALLED IN SICK TO WORK SO WE could stay in bed and spend the morning and perhaps even a portion of the afternoon doing that whole "your body is a wonderland," "skyrockets-in-flight" thing that married people sometimes do.

DATE _____ 20 _____

THE FIRST TIME ONE OF US REALIZED (MANY DAYS TOO LATE) THAT THERE IS perhaps nothing in the world more permanent and unchangeable than "my side of the bed."

DATE _____ 20 _____

THE FIRST TIME I ACCIDENTALLY USED HER TOOTHBRUSH, STOPPED, AND THEN started brushing again, thinking, "Aw, she's my wife. It doesn't really matter."

DATE _____ 20 _____

THE FIRST TIME WE BOTH REALIZED THE EXTREME GRAVITY OF OUR OFFICIAL commitment when we put each other's name down as "Beneficiary" on our life insurance policy.

DATE _____ 20 _____

PURCHASED AT:

THE FIRST TIME WE HAD A DINNER PARTY (WITH OUR REGISTRY TABLE SETTINGS and everything) and took a moment to notice the occurrence of the social-anthropological phenomenon of gender sifting, in which the men inevitably work their way outside around the grill, while the women work their way inside around the kitchen center island.

DATE   20

THE FIRST TIME WE PUT OURSELVES IN THE PLACE OF VISITORS TO OUR HOME, looked around our house, and decided to scale back the extent of our smiling-couple wedding photos from "outrageously allegiant shrine" to "ridiculous and appalling collection of photographic excess."

DATE   20

THE FIRST TIME I WAS OUT SHOPPING WITH MY WIFE AND WITNESSED ONE
of those gift-registry couples, and saw her scold him for pretending that the
handheld price scanner is a laser pistol, and thought, "That's only the beginning,
my friend."

DATE _____ 20 _____

THE FIRST (AND LAST, OR AT LEAST NEXT-TO-LAST) TIME WE USED OUR
ridiculously expensive, top-of-the-line gift registry bread maker.

DATE _____ 20 _____

THE FIRST TIME WE GOT AN E-MAIL WITH THE SUBJECT HEADING "HOW'S MARRIED life?" from that seemingly nice but alarmingly saccharine newlywed couple (who appeared to like us a little more desperately than we liked them) we were seated beside at dinner on our honeymoon.

DATE _____ 20 _____

THE FIRST TIME WE GOT A KNOCK ON OUR DOOR FROM THAT SEEMINGLY NICE but-not-really-daily-hang-out-material newlywed couple that was "Ha-ha! Surprise!" in town for a long weekend.

DATE _____ 20 _____

1

DATE: INT: ●   INT: ●

2

DATE: INT: ●   INT: ●

3

DATE: INT: ●   INT: ●

4

DATE: INT: ●   INT: ●

5

DATE: INT: ●   INT: ●

MARRIAGE-CONTRACT ADDITIONS AND AMENDMENTS

THE FIRST TIME WE SAT DOWN AND BROKERED A PERMANENT AND BINDING couplehood contract that appointed equally abominable household chores, as in, "Okay, if you agree to always clean up the cat vomit, I'll promise to always address and sign all the holiday cards."

DATE _____ 20 _____

THE FIRST TIME WE ENGAGED IN THE PRAXIS BARTER SYSTEM OF RELATIONSHIP survival, in which one of us agrees to give up, say, drywall-cracking belches if the other agrees to, say, cease all attempts at full-light-of-day, public, spousal zit squeezing.

DATE _____ 20 _____

THE FIRST TIME WE ENGAGED IN NEW-ADULT-LIFE FURNITURE CLEANSING
(i.e., upgrading from his "found" large, wooden cable-spool coffee table to a more respectable, store-bought one).

DATE _____ 20 _____

THE FIRST TIME ONE OF US WAS ABLE TO TRUTHFULLY USE THE ALL-POWERFUL
salesperson-conversation ender, "I'll have to check with my spouse."

DATE _____ 20 _____

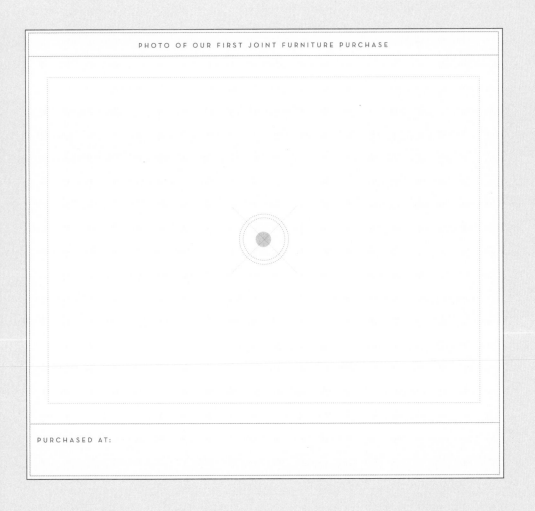

PHOTO OF OUR FIRST JOINT FURNITURE PURCHASE

PURCHASED AT:

THE FIRST (AND LAST, OR AT LEAST NEXT-TO-LAST) TIME WE USED OUR
ridiculously expensive, top-of-the-gift-registry KitchenAid mixer.

DATE   20

THE FIRST TIME A CLOSE FRIEND MADE THE OBSERVATION THAT I HAD
unconsciously commandeered (and taken for my own) one of my spouse's trademark
phrases.

DATE   20

THE FIRST TIME I REALIZED THAT SHOUT-SINGING, IN AN UMBRELLA-DRINK-
addled stupor, all the words to "I Will Survive" is something I will never, ever, ever
have to do again.

DATE _____ 20 _____

THE FIRST TIME I WAS OUT AT A BAR AND REALIZED THERE ARE INDEED SOME
frisky women who love married guys, but those women are the ones you usually
see on *Cops* with a cigarette sticking to their bottom lip while they cuss out a
police officer.

DATE _____ 20 _____

THE FIRST TIME WE REALIZED WE NEVER WROTE A WEDDING-GIFT THANK-YOU note to someone we were about to see the next day.

DATE _____ 20 _____

THE FIRST TIME WE REGIFTED ONE OF OUR WEDDING GIFTS BECAUSE WE HAVE no use for a hanging, handcrafted, wooden bird whose wings flap when you pull the string, but Ted and Alice certainly do.

DATE _____ 20 _____

THE FIRST TIME MY STILL-SINGLE FRIENDS, WHILE IN AN UMBRELLA-DRINK-addled stupor, bestowed upon my husband that most honored and highest compliment of all time: "I just want to find a man like yours."

DATE _____ 20 _____

THE FIRST TIME ONE OF US REALIZED WE HAD FORGOTTEN TO CANCEL OUR online personals ad after receiving a random response from "Sensitive Fireman Guy" or "Girl Just Wants to Have Fun" in our e-mail in-box.

DATE _____ 20 _____

PHOTO OF NEW "FRIENDS" FROM HONEYMOON

LEFT TO RIGHT:

THE TIME WE HAD OUR FIRST MARRIED-COUPLE ARGUMENT.

The topic:

DATE _____ 20 _____

THE FIRST TIME WE FOLLOWED THE AFOREMENTIONED ARGUMENT WITH LIGHT-dimming, neighbor-waking, "we should argue more often" makeup sex.

DATE _____ 20 _____

THE FIRST TIME I WAS SUMMONED TO THE BEDROOM
by my full married name.

DATE _____ 20 _____

THE FIRST TIME WE SAT DOWN AND BROKERED A PERMANENT AND BINDING
amendment to the monogamy section of our married contract to permit each of us
to engage in sexual congress with one unvetoable celebrity of our choosing (assum-
ing, of course, that the moment would somehow divinely present itself). And, no,
the Olsen twins do not count as one.

DATE _____ 20 _____

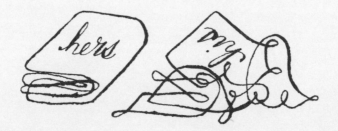

THE FIRST TIME I NOTICED A PILE OF HIS DISCARDED DIRTY CLOTHES ON THE floor and unconsciously snapped something like, "Honey, cleanliness is what separates us from the animals," only to realize I sounded just like my mother.

DATE _____ 20 _____

THE FIRST TIME I DID SOMETHING NORMAL (LIKE PAINT MY FACE BLUE AND GOLD during the Michigan game or sit down to eat a bowlful of cereal endorsed by cartoon characters), only to have her say something disapproving such as, "C'mon honey, no, we're married now."

DATE _____ 20 _____

THE FIRST TIME WE REFERRED TO EACH OTHER AS "HUSBAND" AND "WIFE"
in public without feeling like we were playing make-believe.

DATE _____ 20 _____

THE FIRST TIME WE REALIZED THAT A NIGHT AT HOME WITH JUST EACH OTHER,
on the couch, watching the premium cable channels is sometimes surprisingly more
fun than going out, trying to find parking, and having our shoes stick to the floor
of an underlit, smoke-filled bar. Not always, but sometimes.

DATE _____ 20 _____

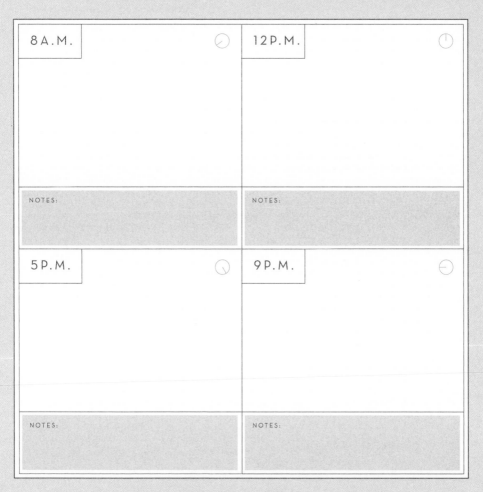

8 A.M.	12 P.M.
NOTES:	NOTES:

5 P.M.	9 P.M.
NOTES:	NOTES:

FIRST VALENTINE'S DAY

THE FIRST TIME WE WERE WALKING OUT OF THE HOUSE AND REALIZED WE WERE dressed exactly alike (meaning, if nothing is done about it, we're only a few years away from purposefully wearing matching sweat suits on airplane flights).

DATE _____ 20 _____

THE FIRST TIME WE WATCHED THE SHOCKING, BICKERING MARRIED COUPLES ON Jerry Springer and asked (mostly comically), "So, whaddaya give us—three, four years before we're like that?"

DATE _____ 20 _____

THE FIRST TIME ONE OF US REFERENCED OUR WEDDING VOWS
during an argument.

DATE _____ 20 _____

THE FIRST TIME MY SPOUSE CAUGHT ME TAKING A LONG, HARD, QUIET LOOK AND
asked, "What?" to which I answered by rote, "Nothing."

DATE _____ 20 _____

THE FIRST TIME ONE OF US EXPOSED OUR HAND IN REGARD TO POSSIBLE future baby names, only to have the other person rip off a nonsensical rant about how "no one ever names their kid Henry, because, before you know it, he's Hank. Then he's Hank the Tank, and that leaves a very narrow career path that includes either managing a fish store or professional wrestling."

DATE _____ 20 _____

···
···
···

THE FIRST TIME ONE OF US TOOK A LONG, HARD, QUIET INTROSPECTIVE LOOK at the other and tried to determine what our kids would look like.

DATE _____ 20 _____

···
···
···

Romeo
Butch
Fanny
Prissy
Candy

THE FIRST TIME HE CEREMONIOUSLY UNEARTHED AND BOXED UP HIS SECRET adult-videotape collection to be donated to his remaining single friend, because he "certainly won't be needing these anymore."

DATE _____ 20 _____

THE FIRST TIME SHE FOUND THE RESERVE, HOLDOUT STASH OF MY ADULT-FILM collection after the apparent, ceremonious "Well, that's the last of them" donation to my single friend.

DATE _____ 20 _____

THE FIRST TIME WE SAT AND POSED FOR OUR VERY FIRST HOLIDAY-CARD PHOTO
(to be accompanied by an exclamation-point-addled "family update" form letter
that will most certainly begin, "Wow!!! What a Year!!!")

DATE _____ 20 _____

THE FIRST TIME I WAS ABLE TO FEND OFF THE UNDESIRABLE ADVANCES OF A
pompous, hair-producted, professional gasbag with the universal, silent-but-deadly,
thumb-on-the-back-of-the-ring-finger "I'm taken" wedding-band wiggle.

DATE _____ 20 _____

NAME:

THE FIRST TIME WE REALIZED WE HAD DEVELOPED WEDDING-RING TAN LINES— a sort of wedding tribal tattoo that makes us clan members (well, at least until summer's over).

DATE _____ 20 _____

THE FIRST TIME WE BABYSAT THE NEPHEWS FOR A LONG, TRIAL WEEKEND, ONLY to realize that, "Yes, one day we'll have kids and be responsible all the time and buy a sensible car and a Family Patriot Pass to Colonial Williamsburg—but thank goodness for the miracle of birth control, that day is not today."

DATE _____ 20 _____

059

THE FIRST TIME I TRULY REALIZED THAT EVEN THOUGH SHE'S NOT PERFECT—
even though she buys way too many houseplants that don't make it, and even
though she doesn't get the male concept of a favorite shirt, and even though she'll
never fully understand the beauty of a 3-6-1 double play—I really do adore everything about her.

DATE _____ 20 _____

....

....

....

....

060

THE FIRST TIME I TRULY REALIZED THAT EVEN THOUGH HE'S NOT PERFECT—
even though he often has just the front part of his shirt tucked in when he leaves
the bathroom, and even though he dances like a man trying to step on a roll-away
quarter, and even though he says "expresso" instead of "espresso"—I really do adore
everything about him.

DATE _____ 20 _____

....

....

....

....

CONTENTS: